A Priceless Princess

CW01656635

A Priceless Princess

Love notes to a daughter
by Nasiroh Omar.

Bismillahir Rahmanir Raheem

Greenbird Books

London

First published in Great Britain in 2012 by Greenbird Books
Text © 2012 by Nasiroh Omar
Cover Art © 2012 by Azra Momin
Graphics © 2012 EclectiCollections
This book has been typeset in Adobe Caslon Pro
Printed in USA
All rights reserved.
No part of this book may be
reproduced, transmitted, or stored in any information
retrieval system in any form or by any means,
graphic, electronic or mechanical, including
photocopying, taping and recording,
without prior written permission from the publisher.
British Library Cataloguing in Publication Data:
A catalogue record for this book is available from the
British Library.

ISBN:978-0-9571995-3-8

www.greenbirdbooks.com

To my priceless princesses,
Anis Sofia,
Anis Aufa,
Anis Alia.

Special thanks to my husband (Afifi),
mother (Minah)
and my boys (Alif and Akif)
for your love and support.

CONTENTS

Acknowledgements

Praise be to Allah, the Most Gracious, the Most Merciful . For in His will I am able to be where I am today. Peace be upon our Prophet Muhammad *SAW*, Allah's messenger, the Praised One. I would like to express my deepest thanks to my beloved husband and family for their never ending love and support in helping me achieve my dreams. Thank you to Greenbird Books for all of their efforts in making this book a reality for an ordinary person like me. A special thank you to my daughter, Anis Sofia for her continuous help and support throughout the whole writing process and making it a meaningful experience. I hope this book will inspire girls all over the world in making their dreams come true, but most importantly, to achieve success in life as a true Muslim. Truly, each and every girl is a priceless princess.

Preface

This book is written by me, a Muslim mother for my daughter whom I called *A Priceless Princess.* Why? Because in Islam a daughter is a priceless gift from Allah (God). A daughter is considered as part of our everlasting treasure, not only for the life in this world but also for the life of the Hereafter. Whatever she did in the past, present and will do in the future contributes as rewards or sins to her parents. Knowing the responsibility of having a daughter, I'm constantly worried about what challenges she will face. Will she be a successful Muslimah? Will she achieve a good balance not only in this world but in the world Hereafter? As time flies, she will grow and lead her own life. So I decided to follow her anywhere and at any time ... with a collection of my *love notes*. I pray other mothers and carers will find some comfort in my words and use this book as a precious gift for their own *priceless princesses*, *Insha Allah*.

Who is it for? For parents and Islamic educators who are looking to impart useful reminders to growing children. The book contains many direct quotes from the Holy Qu'raan. Muslims refer to the Qu'raan and Hadith for all matters of guidance. Throughout our lives, we are all constantly tested with challenges and even blessings! The main message from this book is to show young Muslim girls how we can refer to the Qur'aan at anytime and reflect on the messages given. This book will hopefully guide them, no matter what the circumstances are, *Insha Allah*.

MORE ABOUT THE AUTHOR...

Nasiroh Omar is a proud Malaysian and has had an ambition to become a credible writer for the past two decades. As a working mother and housewife, she spent her only free time writing books that were inspired by her children. Her ideas also developed from reading the passages from the Qur'aan.

After earning a computer science degree from Binghamton University, USA and her masters from University Kebangsaan Malaysia, she lived in England for five years with her family and later earned a PhD from the University of Nottingham, UK. The author then returned to her home country and pursued a career as a senior lecturer from the Faculty of Computer and Mathematical Sciences at the Universiti Teknologi MARA, Malaysia. Currently, her special interests in research involves quantification of virtual user's understanding in task-based events. The author now lives in Shah Alam, Selangor, Malaysia with her husband and five children, where she is busy at work on her next book.

Opening Note

My Dear Priceless Princess,

I am presenting you with this book as a gift. It is a compilation of love notes written by a mother for her daughter as she grew up. I think it's time for me to share them with you now. I hope these notes will help you in many ways and hopefully, you will treasure them forever ...

I will always be praying for your happiness in both worlds: this world and the Hereafter.

Loving you always,

Mom

1

Love Note # 1: From Where to Where?

Dear Priceless Princess,

This is the first of many love notes that I am writing to you. This is the most important note and you have to keep it close to your heart. Of course, I hope that my words become your words and are passed on through future generations bound in love for all that is sacred. Know that when I am gone I will continue to receive a portion of rewards or sins based on your life and the same applies to you should you have a family *Insha Allah*.

Being a Muslim and a mother I have to make sure that you are on a righteous Islamic path, this path if carefully prepared now can be followed by many a Muslimah after us. Let me begin with reminding you about the nature of a human being's journey as prescribed by *Allah SWT*.

Who is Allah SWT?

Allah SWT is the one and only God. There is no god except *Allah SWT*. This acknowledgement is the first and foremost significant belief for Muslims. *Allah SWT* is our Creator and it is He who created us. He draws a standard journey for all human beings including you and me. Let us start from the beginning of our existence.

We start the journey as a spirit who lives in a spiritual world. For how long have we stayed in this spiritual world? Only *Allah SWT* knows the answer. After that stage, *Allah SWT* places us in our mother's tummy as a tiny baby. We stay in our mother's womb for nine months, constantly growing and sleeping peacefully. Babies cannot remember what it was like in their mother's womb. But a mother is aware of tiny kicks and movement; she knows that there is another human life growing inside her.

After nine months of resting in our mother's womb, at last we are born. From then, our life as a human being begins. This is without doubt the most important phase in our journey. Why? You'll discover the answer as we go along...

When the time comes, we will die. The next chapter of our life begins; life in a cemetery! We stay here until the Day of Resurrection when everything will be destroyed. We cannot do anything in the cemetery but wait until the Day of Resurrection. We will wait for *Allah SWT* to evaluate our deeds. If we have done more good deeds than bad deeds in our lifetime, we will live happily and peacefully in the cemetery.

After the Day of Resurrection, we enter the world of the Hereafter. This is the final stop of our journey. We will live either in Heaven or Hell according to our deeds. Muslims strive to attain Heaven, this is the ultimate place for us to live in. How long will we live there? ABSOLUTELY FOREVER AND EVER! Living without an end. This is the final destination of our existence.

Allah SWT has described the journey of a human being perfectly, from life in the spiritual world to life in the Hereafter, without missing a beat. But sometimes in our busy, occupied life, we seem to forget the aim of our existence. We must not forget, that we were created by *Allah SWT* to do good deeds in this world. Discovery in science has confirmed what *Allah SWT* describes about our standard journey in the Qur'aan.

It is noted that no other scientific finding can contradict this Verse.

"O mankind! If you are in doubt concerning the Resurrection, then We have created you from the dust, then from a drop of seed, then from a clot, then from a little lump of flesh shapely and shapeless, then We make (it) clear for you. And We cause what We will to remain in the wombs for an appointed time, and afterwards We bring you out as an infant, then (give you growth) that you attain your full strength. And among you, he who brought back to the most abject time of life, so that, after knowledge, he knows nothing. And you (Muhammad) see the earth barren, but when We send down water on it, it thrills and swells and put forth every lovely kind of growth." *Surah Al Hajj*, Verse 5.

This verse clearly illustrates the life cycle of a human being:

1. A drop of seed (sperm)
2. A blood clot
3. A little lump of flesh
4. A complete baby
5. An infant
6. A toddler
7. A teenager
8. An adult
9. An elderly

Dear Priceless Princess,

Life in this world has a finite time. Living in the Hereafter is forever. The worst Muslim is the one who goes astray. Thus, our love towards the Hereafter must be far greater than our love for life in this world. Sacrificing our needs in this world for the needs of the Hereafter will benefit us greatly not only for the present but also the eternal future.

I always pray to *Allah SWT* that you and I will never forget the origin of our creation, from a tiny foetus, to a fully-grown human being. Always keep this in the deepest part of your heart that *Allah SWT* has created us without any imperfections. So we must ALWAYS be thankful to *Allah SWT*. Let us show our appreciation by doing good deeds in everything we do.

Forever and always,

Mom

2

Love Note # 2: Life is about Knowing the End points

Dear Priceless Princess,

In our journey of life, a Muslim must believe that there are only two endpoints; Heaven or Hell. We cannot see what Heaven or Hell looks like, because *Allah* SWT has not given us this wisdom. However, some hints are given in the Qur'aan .

What does HEAVEN look like?

Only *Allah* SWT knows what Heaven looks like and therefore it will remain a secret and a surprise for all Muslims. However, *Allah* SWT lets us have a peek of the characteristics of Heaven, described in the Qur'aan and by the prophets. Nevertheless, we are not encouraged to visualize heaven in relation to real-life materials as we do not know what it looks like. The hints are just a reminder for us to decide which type of life in the hereafter we are searching for.

In a sentence from the Qur'aan, *Allah* SWT describes heaven as follows;
"Whoever obeys *Allah* SWT and His messenger, He will make him enter Gardens underneath which rivers flow, where such will dwell forever. That will be the great success." *Surah An Nisa,* Verse 13.

In different verses, *Allah* SWT said; "Their Lord gives them good tidings of mercy from Him, and acceptance, and Gardens where enduring pleasure will be theirs." *Surah At Taubah*, Verse 21.

"And verily in the heaven we have set mansions of the stars, and We have beautified it for beholders." *Surah Al Hijr*, Verse 16.

Allah SWT also gives an overview on the occupants' outfit in Heaven; "Gardens of Eden! They enter them wearing armlets of gold and pearl and their garment in there is silk." *Surah Al Malaikah*, Verse 33.

"As for such, theirs (believers) will be gardens of Eden, in which rivers flow beneath them, in it they will be given armlets of gold and will wear green robes of finest silk and gold embroidery, reclining upon thrones in it. Blessed the reward, and fair the resting-place." *Surah Al Kahf*, Verse 29.

Heaven's description in the glorious Qur'aan

"A similitude of the Garden which is promised to those who keep their duty (to *Allah SWT*): underneath it rivers flow; its food is everlasting, and its shade; this is the reward of those who keep their duty, while the reward of disbelievers is the Fire." *Surah Ar Rad*, Verse 35.

"A similitude of the Garden which those who keep their duty (to) *Allah SWT* are promised. In it there are rivers of unpolluted water, and rivers of milk of which the flavour does not change, and rivers of wine delicious to the drinkers, and rivers of clear-run honey; in it for them every kind of fruit, with pardon from their Lord. (Are those who enjoy all this) like those who are immortal in the Fire and are given boiling water to drink so that it tears their bowels?" *Surah Muhammad*, Verse 15.

What does HELL looks like?

In a sentence in the Qur'aan, *Allah SWT* describes hell as: "And who disobeys *Allah SWT* and His messenger and transgresses His limits, He will make him enter fire, where he will dwell forever, His will be a shameful doom." *Surah An-Nisa*, Verse 14.

"Say: (It is) the truth from the Lord of you (all). Then whoever wills, let him believe, and whoever wills, let him disbelief. We have prepared for disbelievers Fire. Its tent enclosed them? If they ask for shower, they will be showered with water like molten lead which burns the faces. Calamitous the drink and ill the resting-place!" *Surah Bani Israil*, Verse 37.

Dear Priceless Princess, life in Hell sounds miserable and hurtful. Such an unkind life has no ending. Therefore, it is clear that Hell is the place we should try to avoid at all cost. As Muslims, we should always obey what *Allah SWT* has instructed us to do in our lives. *Insh Allah*, we will be rewarded for our good deeds and protected against all evil.

Hell's description in the glorious Qur'aan

Let us take a look at what exists in Hell, as is written in the Qur'aan. We can and shall decide with our deeds.

"To Him is the return of all of you. It is a promise of *Allah SWT* in truth. He produced creation, then reproduces it, that He may reward those who believe and do good works in equity; while as for those who disbelieve, theirs will be a boiling drink and painful doom because they disbelieved." *Surah Yunus*, Verse 4.

Allah SWT said: "Hell is before him (a person), and he (the person) is made to drink a festering (rotten) water, which he sips but can hardly swallow, and death comes to him from every side while yet he cannot die, and before him is a harsh doom." *Surah Ibrahim*, Verses 16-17.

3

Love Note # 3: Life is about Pursuing the Standard Journey

Dear Priceless Princess,

As Muslims we believe in the Hereafter and *Allah* SWT's promise to His followers. Each and every one of us must go through the standard journey. We must aim towards being successful in this world and most importantly in the Hereafter.

Basically, this is the standard journey that we have to follow:

Spiritual

Unborn

This World

Cemetery

Hereafter

Definitely, the condition of our Hereafter life depends on the life in this world. As *Allah* SWT said: "You are repaid nothing except what you did." *Surah As-Saffat*, Verse 37.

"And it is said to those who ward off (evil); What has your Lord revealed? They say: Good. For those who do good in this world there is a good (reward), and the home of the Hereafter will be better. Pleasant indeed will be the home of those who ward off (evil)." *Surah An Nahl*, Verse 30.

Therefore, whatever you do in this world will affect you in the ultimate world of the Hereafter!

4

Love Note # 4: Life is Short!

Dear Priceless Princess,

We both should always remember that whatever happens to us, after we die, totally depends on our deeds in this world. And, that includes whatever we did in the past, what we are doing right now and what we will do in the future.

Our duration of life in this world is short! Much, much shorter than the duration of life in the Hereafter. For instance, a minute on Earth is equivalent to thousands, millions or even billions of years in the Hereafter. When will we die? Only *Allah* SWT knows.

The Prophet Muhammad *SAW* died at the age of 63. A child can die at the age of three. A mother could die in her mid-thirties. People can die at various stages in their life. We do not know when it is our turn. But we do know that we will not live forever. LIFE IS SHORT.

Allah SWT said: "You will die and they will die." *Surah Az-Zumar*, Verse 30. Furthermore, *Allah* SWT also said: "He gives life and gives death, and to HIM you will return." *Surah Yunus*, Verse 56.

Within the limited time of our life, we have to dream, set our goals and strategize on how to make use of our life. Our time on Earth is short and we do not know when we will die. Thus, we should use the time that we have wisely so we could benefit from our deeds in the Hereafter.

5

Love Note # 5: Life is a Duty

Dear Priceless Princess,

Truly, *Allah* SWT did not create us for nothing. *Allah* SWT said: "I created the jinn and humankind only that they might worship Me." *Surah Adh-Dhariyat*, Verse 56.

Each of us has a duty to perform and that is to worship *Allah* SWT, this includes believing in and obeying Him anywhere and at any time. And, *Allah* SWT said: "O you who believe! Be mindful of your duty to *Allah* SWT, and seek the way of approach to Him, and strive in His way in order that you may succeed." *Surah Al-Ma'idah*, Verse 35.

He also said: "And for those who believe and do good works, He will pay them their wages in full. *Allah* SWT loves not wrongdoers." *Surah Al-Imran*, Verse 56.

How do we believe in *Allah* SWT? We must hold on tightly to the six Pillars of Belief. If a Muslim does not believe in all six, then there is no faith.

Pillar of Belief # 1: Belief in Allah *SWT* (God)

There's only one, unique and incomparable God and that is *Allah* SWT. *Allah* SWT has neither children nor partner. He is the only one we can worship and ask for help.

Allah SWT describes Himself as: "Say: He is *Allah* SWT, the One! *Allah* SWT, the eternally implored by all! He begets not nor was He begotten. And there is none comparable to Him." *Surah Al-Ikhlas*, Verses 1:4.

Pillar of Belief # 2: Belief in Angels

What is an angel? An angel is an honoured creature that is not visible to the human eye. An angel worships and obeys *Allah* SWT alone at all times.

Angels only act by *Allah SWT*'s command. Among many, there are ten angels, each with their specific tasks. As a Muslim, it is compulsory for us to remember the ten angels and their duties.

Gabriel – He brought down the Qur'aan to the Prophet Muhammad *SAW*.
Munkar and **Nakir** - They question the dead in their graves.
Azrael – He is responsible for parting the soul from the body.
Maalik - He is the chief of the angels who governs Hell.
Ridwan – He is responsible to guard Heaven.
Raqib and **Atid** - Two of whom are charged with each human being; one writes down good deeds, and the other writes down our evil doings.
Mikhael - He provides nourishments for our bodies and souls.
Israfil - He who will blow the trumpet twice at the end of this world.

Pillar of Belief # 3: Belief in the Prophets

There are twenty-five PROPHETS whom we believe in, starting from the Prophet Adam *AS* and ending with Prophet Muhammad *SAW*. Although they were gifted human beings, none of them had the divine qualities equivalent to *Allah SWT*. Prophets were just special human beings who *Allah SWT* chose to send His orders to mankind.

Muslims are the followers of the last Prophet, Prophet Muhammad *SAW*. As his followers we are encouraged to follow his behaviour and way of life, which is the *Sunnah*, in everyday activities. For this we will be rewarded by *Allah SWT*.

Pillar of Belief # 4: Belief in Allah *SWT* (God's) Revealed Books

For this pillar, a Muslim must believe that *Allah SWT* revealed four Books of Revelations to His messengers. However, the Qur'aan (sometimes referred to as the Reminder), which is revealed to Prophet Muhammad *SAW*, is the last revelation. The contents in the Qur'aan will be guarded till the Day of Judgment, as assured by *Allah SWT*: "We, even We, reveal the Reminder, and We verily are its Guardian." *Surah Al Hijr*, Verse 9.

My Priceless Princess, sometimes you may wonder why we really need the Qur'aan. Have you ever bought a board game or an electronic gadget that did not come with an instruction manual? Why do we need the manuals? We need instructions to guide us so that we can use these things in the correct way in order to function properly. The same goes for human beings! *Allah SWT* is our Creator. He creates us in such a way that we can operate by ourselves. Thus, He sent the Qur'aan for us to refer to as our manual. Follow the Qur'aan and you will be safe in this world and in the Hereafter.

Pillar of Belief # 5: Belief in the Day of Judgment

As Muslims, we must believe that there will be a day when everything will be destroyed, known as the Day of Judgment. This is the day leading up to everything we believe in and the day all our deeds will be assessed.

Pillar of Belief # 6: Belief in Al-Qadr

The last pillar of belief is to believe in *Al-Qadr*. We must believe that the God who created us also creates our Divine Predestination. What is the Divine Predestination? In the simplest of words, it means that everything that has happened in the past, is happening in the present or will happen in the future has already been decided by *Allah SWT*. However, *Allah SWT* has given us the freedom to choose between right or wrong. He also gives us the freewill to succeed or to fail; to do good deeds or to go astray. Our life is our choice. The choice that we continuously make will change our default values – the Divine Predestination (if and only in *Allah SWT*'s will).

Dear Priceless Princess, do you know how to believe in the *Al-Qadr*?

We must believe these facts:

1. *Allah SWT* is the Creator of everything in the whole universe – from the biggest of His creation to the tiniest. Planets, stars, mountains, the sea, the sky and human beings are all examples of *Allah SWT*'s beautiful creations.
2. *Allah SWT* knows everything. That is, He knows what is in the past, present and future. *Allah SWT* also knows the visible and the invisible.
3. *Allah SWT* is recording every single detail of everything that is happening.
4. Everything that happens or does not happen is due to *Allah SWT*'s will. *Allah SWT* is the only one who has the power to decide.

How do we obey *Allah SWT* and carry out our duties as Muslims?

Dear Priceless Princess, to make sure we fulfil all of *Allah SWT*'s commands, we must hold on tightly to the six Pillars of Islam. What do these pillars represent? They are our life's agenda. Throughout our journey of life, these are the major elements that we have to obey in order to complete our duties.

6

Love Note # 6: Life is Like a Game

Dear Priceless Princess,

Life is like a digital game! *Allah SWT* said: "The life of the world is but a sport (game) and a pastime. And if you believe and ward off (evil), He will give your wages, and will not ask of you your worldly wealth." *Surah Muhammad*, Verse 36.

Luckily, you are born in a digital age and are therefore aware of the current advancements in technology. I would like to ask you, how many games have you ever played so far? I'm sure you have spent countless hours in the day playing games online?

One important fact that you should know is that most games share several common characteristics:

1. It limits your play time. You have a certain amount of time to achieve the goal of the game.

2. It challenges your skills. You need to use various strategies in order to win the game.

3. It rewards you with points and you can accumulate the points within the specific play time. The more points you gain the better player you become.

4. It deducts your accumulated points if you fail to complete a specific task in the game. The more points you lose, the weaker player you become.

5. It offers you a set of tasks. The purpose of each task in the game is to test your ability and strength, mentally or physically. Every task relates to your achievements, whether you gain or lose points.

6. It categorizes the players into several levels of standings. The higher the level, the better the player. You do know that you are competing against yourself and other players in order to achieve the optimum score or to win the game.

7. Winning the game = SUCCESS = HAPPINESS!

My Priceless Princess, like I said, our life shares many similarities to a game:

1. We are given (by *Allah SWT*) a limited time to live.

2. Living is not an easy process. At any moment, we are expected to act and use various strategies in order to succeed in life.

3. *Allah SWT* rewards us for every good deed and we can accumulate the rewards within our lifetime. The more rewards we gain, the better Muslims we become.

4. When we make a mistake or fail to complete a specific task as prescribed by *Allah SWT* we are incurring sin on ourselves. The more sins we accumulate, the weaker Muslims we become.

5. *Allah SWT* asks for us to perform a set of tasks throughout our lifetime. Every given task is aimed to test our faith towards *Allah SWT*. Every task is associated with whether you gain rewards or sins.

6. *Allah SWT* will categorize us into several levels based on our accumulated rewards and sins. The more rewards we have, the better Muslims we are. The more sins we have, the worse Muslims we are. We are competing against ourselves in order to achieve the highest prize, which is Paradise.

7. Winning the game of life = SUCCESS = HEAVEN! In *Allah SWT*'s will.

7

Love Note # 7: How to Gain Rewards and Avoid Sins

Dear Priceless Princess,

In Islam, human action can be classified into five categories:

Wajib (compulsory). All actions under this category must be performed by a Muslim at any cost, unless we are not mature, unconscious or retarded. Example: It is compulsory to pray five times a day. Doing the *wajib* act, we gain rewards. Neglecting the *wajib* act, we gain sins.

Haram (forbidden). All actions under this category should be avoided by a Muslim at any cost unless we are not mature, unconscious, retarded or in an emergency. For example, we are forbidden to consume alcohol or any product that contains alcohol. Doing the *haram* act, we gain sins neglecting the *haram* act, we gain rewards.

Sunnah (encouraged). Muslims are encouraged to perform all actions under this category. For example, smiling is an act of *sunnah*. Doing the *sunnah* act, we gain rewards Neglecting the *sunnah* act, we gain nothing.

Makruh (discouraged). Muslims are discouraged to perform all actions under this category. Example: Eating smelly food is a *makruh* act. Avoiding the *makruh* act, we gain rewards Doing the *makruh* act, we gain nothing.

Mubah (neutral). This act is neither forbidden nor recommended. Muslims are free to do or avoid such acts. Example: Daily activities such as eating and sleeping. It is okay for us to do or avoid any act under this category. No rewards or sins are involved here.

What is meant by an act? An act is anything that a human being can do either physically or mentally, be it visible or invisible to human beings, seen or unseen by any human being, for example, you may see a boy kicking a cat. The act of kicking is physical since the boy uses his leg to kick. The action is visible because we can see the kicking motion.

The action is seen, because there are people who witnessed it.

What about the action of a thief who intends to steal somebody's money? Of course, we cannot see his act of thinking. Thus, his action in this case is invisible to other people and hence the act of thinking is unseen.

Another example of an act is a man punching a person. His action of punching is visible because people can see that he has used his hand to punch. However, nobody else had witnessed him punching the person, therefore, is unseen by other people.

Dear daughter, *Allah* SWT is the All-Seeing and All-Hearing, so whether one commits an act or thinks of one it does not matter because *Allah* SWT will always know of it. As Muslims we believe in our hearts that *Allah* SWT is always evaluating our acts whether they are visible or invisible, seen or unseen! Next time you are about to do something, always think about *Allah* SWT's evaluation first.

8

Love Note # 8: Life is about Winning a Game

Dear Priceless Princess,

As you know, our life resembles a game, where we as the players are required to achieve a certain goal. The prize for winning this game is either getting a life of peace and contentment or suffering and pain.

The big question is; how do we win this game of life? The strategy to win this game is to gain as much rewards as possible and to always avoid any sins.

Allah SWT said: "That *Allah* SWT may reward them with the best of what they did, and increase reward for them of His Bounty, *Allah* SWT gives blessings without limit to whom He wills." *Surah An-Nur*, Verse 38.

You must always keep in mind that *Allah* SWT is the MOST MERCIFUL. For some of our good actions, He multiplies our rewards. For example, we will get twenty-seven times more rewards if we perform our prayer along with a group of other people than if we pray alone.

So, within our limited lifetime, we must STRIVE to get more rewards by doing the *Wajib* (compulsory) and *Sunnah* (encouraged) actions only. Avoid at all cost the *Haram* (forbidden) and *makruh* (discouraged) actions.

Insha-*Allah* SWT, during the Day of Judgment, the day when *Allah* SWT weighs our rewards and sins, our rewards weigh a lot more than our sins. The best case is when there are no sins at all – that is surely the greatest achievement, if *Allah* SWT wills.

Allah SWT said: "And We set a just balance for the Day of Resurrection so that no soul is wronged in anything. Though it be of the weight of a grain of mustard seed. We bring it. And We suffice for reckoners." *Surah Al-Anbiya*, Verse 47.

Allah SWT also said: "Those whose scales are heavy, they are the successful." *Surah Al-Mu'kminun*, Verse 102.

9

Love Note # 9: Allah swt has the Greatest CCTV

Dear Priceless Princess,

Do you know what a CCTV is?

CCTV is an acronym for Closed Circuit Television. It is a television-like device which uses a video camera to record, controlled by a computer. Usually, the device is hidden somewhere to record activities for a specific surrounding. Living in this digital age, you must have come across a lot of CCTVs in your lifetime. Have you ever seen a sign that reads, "There is a hidden camera in this area," or "Beware of CCTV"? This means that there is a camera nearby recording your every move! In simpler words, it is a computerized watchdog.

Normally, people or organizations such as banks, shops or even houses have some form of surveillance for the purpose of recording any activities within their territories. In case of unwanted robbers or intruders who enter their territories, it is able to capture and record their suspicious behaviours. Hopefully, by recording the surrounding activities, the police or owners of the building might find clues to detect the intruders' activities.

Even so, this device is not 100% reliable. Most of the current versions have limited capabilities. Since it captures intruders from a distance, the captured images are sometimes blurry. It records only in the form of movements or postures of intruders but not their thoughts or speech. Yet, whenever we see either the camera itself or just the sign of its existence, we are careful of our actions because we are conscious of being watched.

As Muslims, are we aware that *Allah swt* is also watching over us? He is watching us twenty-four-seven. Is this possible? Definitely, the answer is yes! *Allah swt* has the greatest and most optimum CCTV.

Always be aware that *Allah swt*'s CCTV is able to capture every action of every living and non-living thing on this earth and beyond.

Allah SWT's CCTV is surely incomparable to the CCTV in this world. It captures more than just a combination of text, image and audio.

Allah SWT describes His CCTV in this Verse "And you (Muhammad) are not occupied with any business and you recite not a Lecture from this Scripture, and you (mankind) perform no act, but We are Witness of you when you are engaged in it. Not an atom's weight in the earth or in the sky escapes your Lord, nor what is less than that or greater than that, but it is (written) in a clear Book." *Surah Yunus*, Verse 61.

Allah SWT also reminds us: "And say (to) them. Act! *Allah SWT* will behold your actions, and (so will) His messenger and the believers, and you will be brought back to the Knower of the Invisible and the Visible, and He will tell you what you used to do." *Surah At Taubah*, Verse 105.

Allah SWT's monitoring is much more complex than the human CCTV. He is able to record anything for all living and non-living things at any time. He records all your actions: invisible or visible, seen or unseen. He keeps a record of all your footprints, speech, thoughts, emotions, goals, aims, ambitions, dreams and everything else. That includes everything in your past, present and future! *Allah SWT*'s knows everything about us.

Again, *Allah SWT* said: "He is *Allah SWT* in the heavens and in the earth. He knows both your secret and your utterance, and He knows what you earn." *Surah Al-An'am*, Verse 3.

"And *Allah SWT* knows that which you keep hidden and that which you proclaim." *Surah An-Nahl*, Verse 19.

My dear Priceless Princess,

Read what *Allah SWT* said: "And with HIM are the keys of the Invisible. None but He knows them. And He knows what is in the land and the sea. Not a leaf falls but He knows it, not a grain in amid (the middle of) the darkness of the earth, nothing of wet or dry but (it is noted) in a clear record." *Surah Al-An'am*, Verse 59.

"Or think ye that ye Shall be abandoned, as though Allah did not know those among you who strive with might and main, and take none for friends and protectors except Allah, His Messenger and the (community of) Believers? But Allah is well-acquainted with (all) that ye do." *Surah At Taubah*, Verse 16.

Another sign of *Allah SWT*'s powerful CCTV is stated in this Verse "Know they not that *Allah SWT* knows both their secret and the thought they confide, and that *Allah SWT* is the Knower of Things Hidden?" *Surah At Taubah*, Verse 78.

"*Allah SWT* is the Knower of the Unseen of the heavens, and the earth. He is

Aware of the secret of (men's) hearts." *Surah Al-Mala'ikah*, Verse 38.

Ultimately, *Allah* SWT said: "And *Allah* SWT knows that which you keep hidden and that which you proclaim." *Surah An-Nahl*, Verse 19.

Hence, remember this; Watch out for *Allah* SWT's CCTV! Always think about your actions and their evaluations. Be the very best of the believers.

10

Love Note # 10: Allah swt has the Greatest Database

Dear Priceless Princess,

Do you know what a database is?

A database is a collection of specific records or information, for example, a collection of information about a student's or a worker's details. Years ago, when there were only a few computers available and they were very expensive, companies or organizations kept their information in the form of paper-based files. Thus, a database is a stack of important files at an office! Can you imagine how difficult it is in order to retrieve one's information from such database?

In this modern age, the use of paper-based files are diminishing. Technology offers a digital type of database. With the help of advanced computers, the data from a database can be stored or retrieved faster than before and uses less space.

A database can store the name, gender, birth date, and identification number of every single person in a country! Advanced technology has taken social networking to a whole new level with applications such as *Facebook*, *Twitter* or *Skype*. Your profile information can easily be stored in the application's database. However, can the database know little details such as what you have eaten last night or that you have lost your money last week? No, the database is only able to record certain information about you and is very limited. There is no database in the world that can be compared to *Allah* SWT's limitless database.

So you see, the database that exists today has many disadvantages. Not only is the information kept and its capabilities limited, but also any database is prone to be corrupted or damaged. It can also be easily hacked, manipulated, stolen, deleted or modified by other people in this world.

Allah SWT reminds us about His greatest database, a database that can never be produced by any brilliant scientist:

"Nor spend they any spending, small or great, nor do they cross a valley, but it is recorded for them, that *Allah SWT* may repay them the best of what they used to do." *Surah At Taubah*, Verse 121.

Allah SWT's database can record all data related to your accountings. Everything you did for every second of your lifetime, all will be recorded! There's no problem of limited storage or issue of who will jot down the details for Him.

"It is We who bring the dead to life. We record that which they send before (them) and their footprints. And all things We have kept in a clear Register." *Surah Ya Sin*, Verse 12.

Acknowledge *Allah SWT*'s greatest database. Nothing can escape from it!

11

Love Note # 11: Life is Multi-Level Marketing

Dearest Priceless Princess,

There is a reason why I am so concerned about what you do in your life and what kind of Muslim you will grow up to be. I want to make sure you try your best in everything you do. Whatever you do contributes to your parents, whether it is rewards or sins. However, there is a strategy to gain the best in life, Multi-Level Marketing.

Do you know what Multi-Level Marketing is? It is a strategy used in business to overcome the challenges in economy. In this modern world, you can gain more money not only when you sell things but also if other people in your group sell the product too. It is a matter of teamwork to be able to sell and make more money. The more people you recruit in your group to sell things, the more profit you will gain!

Life in this world is like Multi-Level Marketing. Muslims believe that when they die, the death is the time border when they cannot directly gain any rewards or sins from *Allah* SWT anymore. That is the ending point of collecting rewards except from three acts that *Allah* SWT allows. Muslims can still receive rewards even after they die, based on:

- Their children's acts, when they gain rewards for doing good.
- Their evergreen charities (their on-going charities).
- Their knowledge that they have passed to other people when they were alive and the people are practising the knowledge given.

Allah SWT said: "And they who believe and whose seed follow them in faith, We cause their seed to join them (there – in Heaven), and We deprive them of nothing of their (life's) work. Every man is a pledge for that which he has earned." *Surah At-Tur*, Verse 21.

So you see, by doing good deeds in a Multi Level Marketing method, we can easily gain continuous profit, *Subhanallah!*

My beloved daughter, please remember to pass these notes to your future children, your future grandchildren and so on. By doing so, you, me and Dad are able to receive three exceptional rewards as I described before in the life Hereafter. Insha-*Allah* SWT.

12

Love Note # 12: Life is a Series of Assessments

Dear Priceless Princess,

Have you ever taken an exam or test in school? I'm pretty sure you have many times! Do you know what is the purpose of an assessment? How does an exam or a test relate to life?

Assessment is very much related to learning. An assessment is used to measure or diagnose how much has been learned by an individual. By adapting a specific type of assessment, teachers gain meaningful insights of the students' performance. On the other hand, students gain self-awareness of their own performance and motivation to keep on learning.

Normally, for every assessment, students are trained to prepare on how to answer the questions. Questions are arranged and formatted in such a way that students are familiar with the format. Thus, they are well prepared!

My dear Priceless Princess, do you realize that our life is a series of assessments? At any time, *Allah* SWT can test us. Most of the time, we are unprepared!

Allah SWT said: "Do men imagine that they will be left (at ease) because they say, 'We believe', and will not be tested with affliction (problems / burdens / difficulties)?"
Surah Al-Ankabut, Verse 2.

Why must *Allah* SWT test us in our life? What is the real purpose?

Allah SWT also said: "We tested those who were before you. Thus *Allah* SWT knows who are sincere, and He knows those who pretend." *Surah Al-Ankabut*, Verse 4.

Allah SWT assesses us because He wants to measure our faith. However, *Allah* SWT's assessments are in various forms and do not have a specific format.

Allah SWT gives an example of the common scope where a human being will be tested: "And know that your possessions and your children are a test, and that with *Allah SWT* is immense reward." *Surah Al-Anfal*, Verse 28.

In any scope in which *Allah SWT* tests us, we have to remember that He is measuring our faith. He can test us in the form of money, sickness, happiness, accidents, friends, enemies and much more!

Unfortunately, we cannot answer His questions in the form of multiple choice or essay. We must use our mental and physical ability to answer *Allah SWT*'s tests patiently and faithfully.

By knowing the fact that *Allah SWT* will test us, let us recite this *dua* again and again. Hopefully, when *Allah SWT* wants to assess our faith in Him, He always has His Mercy on us:

"*Allah SWT* tasks not a soul beyond its scope. For it (is) only that which it has earned, and against it (only) that which it has deserved. Our Lord! Condemn us not if we forget, or miss the mark! Our Lord! Lay not on us such a Burden as you did on those before us! Our Lord! Impose not on us that which we have not the Strength to Bear! Pardon us and Absolve us and have Mercy on us, You our Protector and give us Victory over the Disbelieving." *Surah Al-Baqarah*, Verse 286.

13

Love Note # 13: Life is about Showing your Love to your Parents

Dear Priceless Princess,

It is compulsory for all of us to be kind to our parents. You can commit a sin towards your parents just by using the wrong tone in your voice.

Remember, *Allah* SWT said: "We have enjoined on man kindness to parents; but if they strive to make you join with Me that of which you have no knowledge, then obey them not. To me is your return and I shall tell you what you used to do." *Surah Al-Ankabut*, Verse 8.

Parents and carers will always remember the feeling of love towards their young infant long after they grow up.

Do remember the following words of *Allah* SWT: "And We have commended to man kindness towards parents. His mother bears him with reluctance, and brings him out with reluctance, and the bearing of him and the weaning of him in thirty months, till, when he attains full strength and reaches forty years, he says: My Lord! Cause me to give thanks for the favour with which You have favoured me and my parents, and that I may do what is right and acceptable to You. And be gracious to me in the matter of my seed. I have turned to You repentant, and I am of those who surrender to you." *Surah Al-Ahqaf*, Verse 15.

14

Love Note # 14: Life is a Multi-tasking Challenge

Dear Priceless Princess,

Life is a multi-tasking challenge. What is multi-tasking, you may wonder? The word multi-tasking is also defined as CPU (Central Processing Unit) which consists of a computer that can complete or execute instructions simultaneously. Imagine that you are working on a computer: you are typing out an essay when at the same time, you are also writing an email in a different window. You use the computer to chat online with your friends from school whilst searching for some information on the Internet. To computer users like us, it seems like all technological gadgets perform tasks simultaneously. But behind the scenes, the CPU has to switch between the tasks and perform each of them in a slice of time.

Truly, our life is also a multi-tasking challenge. Why? Because, in this one and only life that has been given by *Allah SWT* to us, we are struggling to complete several tasks or duties for two worlds: this world and the Hereafter. At any given time, we will perform an action. The action can be targeted to gain rewards from *Allah SWT* for the Hereafter or for the purpose of a better life in this world.

Our life looks as if two categories of tasks are running simultaneously. On one side, we are trying to achieve the best for the purpose of living in this world. On the other side, we are also are trying our hardest for the purpose of living in the Hereafter.

All of our actions can be classified into three categories:

- solely for the purpose of life in this world
- solely for the purpose of life in the Hereafter
- for the purpose in both worlds: this world and the Hereafter

Believe it or not, every moment of a true Muslim's life, they are doing a multi-tasking job; balancing between accomplishing the best life in this world and the Hereafter.

Each of our acts will fall into any of the three categories depending on our intention. For example: You want to study because you want to get a good job. Hence, it is only for the success in this world. But how will that prepare you for the Hereafter?

Allah SWT said: "And when you have completed your devotions, then remember *Allah SWT* as you remember your fathers or with a more lively remembrance. But the mankind is he who says: 'Our Lord! Give to us in the world,' and he has no portion in the Hereafter." *Surah Al-Baqarah*, Verse 200.

If you say that you want to study because of *Allah SWT* and also to get a good job, then the act of your study benefits yourself for both worlds: the Hereafter and this world. Hence, you will be considered as a winner in both worlds.

Allah SWT wants us to do things that are beneficial in both worlds. As *Allah SWT* said: "And of them (also) is he who says, 'Our Lord! Give to us in this world that which is good and in the Hereafter that which is good, and guard us from the doom of Fire. For them there is in store a goodly portion out of that which they have earned. *Allah SWT* is swift at reckoning." *Surah Al-Baqarah*, Verses: 201-202.

Nevertheless, if you say you only want to do good to gain rewards for the Hereafter only, then you will have to answer for your wordly contributions!

Make sure you aim to succeed in both worlds; this is what *Allah SWT* wants for all Muslims. Become a person who balances their tasks in life, surely you will gain rewards in both worlds – Insha-*Allah SWT*.

15

Love Note # 15: Life is a Concurrent System

Dear Priceless Princess,

Do you realize that our life is a concurrent system? What exactly is meant by concurrent system? In today's modern age, the term concurrent system is referred to as a system in which multiple tasks are carried out at the same time, interweaving with each other.

Our life in this world is equivalent to a concurrent system. Let's assume that we are systems. How many tasks must we perform throughout our life in this world?

Just take me as an example:

- I'm a Muslim – thus I have to perform all my duties as a Muslim.
- I'm a follower of the Prophet Muhammad *SAW* – thus, I have to try my best to follow his behaviour and actions.
- I'm a citizen – thus I have to perform all duties that a citizen should do.
- I'm a daughter – hence, I have to fulfil my duty as a daughter. Obey my parents, respect my parents, take care of them if they were sick etc.
- I'm a wife to my husband – thus, I have duties to fulfil as a wife.
- I'm a mother – thus, I must carry out my responsibility as a parent.
- I'm a sister – I must treat my siblings well as a sister.
- I'm a worker to my organization – thus, I have to fulfil all my duties in relation to the post. Attend meetings, prepare reports, respect my fellow co-workers etc.
- I'm a neighbour – I have duties to perform as a neighbour.
- I'm a committee member of an organization – thus, I must take part in the committee activities as a member.

Can we stop some of the tasks that we have to run? It all depends. Compulsory duties such as being a Muslim, a follower of Prophet Muhammad *SAW*, a wife, a mother and a sister is a lifetime responsibility in nature. Nevertheless, I can stop being a worker if I resign from the job. The main point is, we are never free from having to carry out a specific duty, and therefore we must do our best in achieving our goals.

In a nutshell, this is a reminder for both you and me. Every once in a while, we should sit down and evaluate ourselves. Have we fulfilled all the tasks for each of our duties? Truly, *Allah SWT* will ask us on the Day of Judgment! Our mouth, ears, hands, legs, eyes and all the organs in our body will be the witness of our deeds. There's nothing we can hide from *Allah SWT*'s CCTV and everything is recorded in His database.

16

Love Note # 16: Life is about Abiding by the Muslims' Clothing Code

Dear Priceless Princess,

When I think about the biggest obstacle to overcome in being a practicing Muslim, the clothing aspect for both men and women is so important. Nowadays, it's normal for Muslim girls to go out in public wearing revealing clothing. You must remember that covering your body in public is compulsory for all Muslim girls. We have a clothing code not only for five times a day (the same as prayer), once a year (like fasting in the month of Ramadan), or once in a lifetime (like performing *Hajj)*, but it is a must for your everyday routine. It is one of the most important duties for a Muslims.

Allah SWT said; "And tell the believing women

- to lower their gaze and be modest,
- and to display of their adornment only that which is apparent,
- and to draw their veils over their chests,
- not to reveal their adornment except to their own husbands or fathers or husbands' fathers or their sons, or their brothers or their brothers' sons or sisters' son or their women, or their slaves, or old male attendants who lack vigour, or children who know nothing of women's nakedness.
- And let them not stamp their feet so as to reveal what they hide of their adornment.

And turn to *Allah* SWT together, O believers, in order that you might succeed." *Surah An-Nur*, Verse 31.

In this verse, *Allah* SWT gives Muslim women a trademark. He asks us to relate with the trademark for our own safety.

As *Allah* SWT said: "O Prophet! Tell your wives and your daughters and the women of the believers to draw their cloaks close around them (when they go out). That will be better, so that they may be recognized and not annoyed. *Allah* SWT is ever Forgiving, Merciful." *Surah Al-Ahzab*, Verse 59.

Deciding on what to wear and not to wear is always naturally tough. Furthermore, the ever changing fashion trends always dictate people's choice of clothing. Each and every girl wants to look trendy and contemporary. How are we supposed to deal with this issue?

Just remember that we will live in the Hereafter far longer than in this world. We have to put life in the Hereafter first and always do good deeds so that we will gain rewards from *Allah SWT*. It is not wrong to follow trends in clothing. However, you must be aware of the three clothing rules:

- Your clothes must cover every part of your body except your face and hands.
- Your clothes must not be too tight that people can easily see your body contour.
- Your clothes must not be transparent allowing people to see through them.

Of course, it is in our nature to long for the latest fashion in trend. You can still follow the trends with the condition that you adapt your clothing to the three important rules. Why not get creative by designing your own fashion? Your designs can be stylish yet suitable for Muslim women. There are many successful Muslimah's who have just done making our dress code one to be proud of. Be the designer, not the follower!

17

Love Note # 17: Signs of Allah swt's Existence

Dear Priceless Princess,

We as human beings are not able to see *Allah* swt with our eyes. *Allah* swt has kept His appearance a secret that can only be revealed to those who are faithful to Him. Only those who abide by His commands are qualified to see Him on the Day of Judgement. Nevertheless, *Allah* swt always shows signs of His existence. Those signs are not only stated in the Qur'aan but also proven through nature and scientific explanation. The signs are everywhere, if only we happen to think and realize!

As *Allah* swt said: "Whatever He has created for you in the earth of diverse hues, it is indeed a sign for people who take heed." *Surah An-Nahl*, Verse 13.

"*Allah* swt is He

- Who created the heavens and the earth,
- and causes water to descend from the sky,
- by it producing fruits as food for you,
- and make the ships to be of service to you, that they may run upon the sea at His command,
- and has made of service to you the rivers;
- And makes the sun and the moon, constant in their courses, to be of service to you,
- and has made of service to you the night and the day."
  Surah Ibrahim, Verses: 32-33.

"And He it is

- Who has compelled the sea to be of service so that you can eat fresh meat from there,
- and bring out from there ornaments which you wear.
- And you see the ships ploughing it that you (mankind) may seek of His

Bounty and that perhaps you give thanks." *Surah An-Nahl*, Verse 14.

"And We send

- the winds fertilising,
- and cause water to descend from sky,
- and give it you to drink.
- It is not you who are the holders of the store of it."
  Surah Al Hijr, Verse 22.

"And We have made the sky a roof withheld (from them). Yet they turn away from its signs. And He it is Who created the night and the day, and the sun and the moon. They float, each in an orbit." *Surah Al-Anbiya*, Verses: 32-33.

You have learnt or will learn in the near future in your science class that the wind blows seeds to different places for it to germinate successfully. It can be explained in a science experiment that a seed needs water to grow. Furthermore, the rain also provides water for us to drink from. *Allah SWT* has created the wind and the rivers that provide many benefits to us continuously. If we look around us, there are many more signs that show *Allah SWT* is our sustainer. Thus, *Allah SWT* challenges us to show that we are weak.

Allah SWT tells us that He creates rivers and roads for our means of transportation:
"And He has cast into the earth firm hills that it quake not with you, and streams and roads that you may find a way." *Surah An-Nahl*, Verse 15.

Allah SWT shows us that we can use stars to find our directions: the North, South, East and West: "And landmarks (too), and by the star they find a way." *Surah An-Nahl*, Verse 15.

Allah SWT reminds us that humans are weak. Humans do not have strength to crush the world into pieces. "And walk not in the earth exultant. You cannot split the earth, nor can you stretch to the height of the hills." *Surah Bani Israil*, Verse 37.

Allah SWT asks us to look at the farm animals, such as goats and cows. The animals provide milk, a necessity for growing infants, meat and skin. All of this brings great advantages to us. *Subhanallah!*

"And in the cattle there is a lesson for you. We give you to drink of that which in their bellies, from between the refuse and the blood, pure milk palatable to the drinkers." *Surah An-Nahl*, Verse 66.

Allah SWT also asks us to look around and ponder on the various types, tastes, sizes, colours of fruits. The fruits provide vitamins and fibres which have been proven scientifically to be healthy for us and a source of sustenance to nourish the body.
"And of the fruits of the date-palm, and grapes, from which you derive strong

and (also) good nourishment. In it is indeed a sign for people who have sense." *Surah An-Nahl*, Verse 67.

Another example of one of the signs of *Allah SWT*'s existence is honey. Honey is proven medically to be the most precious food, offering many advantages to the consumer. Among its goodness, honey is easy to digest, it generates heat, replaces energy, helps our body to form important enzymes and kills germs. Honey is made naturally by *Allah SWT*'s command, something mankind cannot create or reproduce, *Subhanallah!*

Allah SWT said: "And your Lord inspired the bee, saying: Choose habitations in the hills and in the tress and in that which they thatch; Then eat of all fruits, and follow the ways of your Lord, made smooth (for you). There comes out from there a drink of diverse hues, in which is healing for mankind. In this is indeed a sign for people who reflect." *Surah An-Nahl*, Verses: 68-69.

Take a look at ourselves and we can find many signs of *Allah SWT*'s existence. Our eyes, ears, nose and mouth all help us to sense things in this world. Imagine if we were born deaf or blind. How do you think you would cope without some or all of your senses by yourself? We must always be thankful to *Allah SWT* for everything he has given us for without it we would be nothing.

"And *Allah SWT* brought you out from the wombs of your mothers knowing nothing, and gave you hearing and sights and hearts, that perhaps you might give thanks." *Surah An-Nahl*, Verse 78.

Birds only fly in the air by *Allah SWT*'s command. Without *Allah SWT*, birds are not able to fly in search of food. These beautiful creatures are another sign of *Allah SWT*'s existence.

As *Allah SWT* said: "Have they not seen the birds obedient in mid air? None hold them except *Allah SWT*. In this, verily are signs for a people who believe." *Surah An-Nahl*, Verse 79.

Moreover, *Allah SWT* also gave us the wisdom to build a house as a shelter as it is a necessity in our lives. It is now clear that nothing is created in this world without a reason. For example, He informs us on how to make use of animals – their meat as our food, their fur for our comfort.

"And *Allah SWT* has given you your houses an abode, and given you (also), of the hides of cattle, houses which you find light (to carry) on the day of migration and on the day of pitching camp; and of their wool and their fur and their hair, an ornament and comfort for a while." *Surah An-Nahl*, Verse 80.

The occurrence of night and day all happen in *Allah SWT*'s will. It is He who commands the sun to rise each morning and to set in the evenings. Mankind rise in the daytime to go in search of income and return home at night to rest after a day's hard work. Truly, we benefit from the occurrence of night and day greatly.

In this verse, *Allah SWT* illustrates how to form a yearly calendar from the presence of night and day: "And We appoint the night and the day two signs. Then We dark the sign of the night, and We make the sign of the day sight-giving, that you may seek bounty from your Lord, and that you may know the computation of years, and the reckoning; and everything We have explained with a clear explanation." *Surah Bani Israil*, Verse 7.

Clearly, the signs of *Allah SWT*'s existence are not limited to those with enough wisdom to look around. Look around the whole universe with your faith and open heart, you will see. If *Allah SWT*'s will. If you happen to see any signs, Insha-*Allah SWT*, you'll see the greatness of your God.

18

Love Note # 18: Life is about Gaining Allah's swt Mercy

Dear Priceless Princess,

Every moment of our life depends on whether we gain *Allah* SWT's mercy or not. If we are able to gain His mercy in our lifetime, we will be safe in the Hereafter, Insha-*Allah* SWT. But how exactly do we gain mercy from the Most Merciful?

In a verse from the Qur'aan, *Allah* SWT said: "And when your Lord proclaimed: If you give thanks, I (*Allah* SWT) will give you more; but if you are thankless, My Punishment is Dire." *Surah Ibrahim*, Verse 7.

And *Allah* SWT also stated: "And He gives you of all you ask of Him, and if you could count the bounty of *Allah* SWT you cannot reckon it. Man is verily wrong-doer, ungrateful." *Surah Ibrahim*, Verse 34.

Have you ever thought about the number of wishes you made that came true? As an example, on such a hot day in the park with your friends, you long for something cold to eat. A moment later, your best friend decides to treat you with an ice cream. I'm quite sure this kind of thing has happened many times before! Truly, *Allah* SWT has granted most of your requests, whether it's big or small. We must always be grateful and give thanks to *Allah* SWT.

My daughter, never forget to say thank you to *Allah* SWT and fill your day with praises for your Lord. Insha-*Allah* SWT we are able to gain His Mercy as *Allah* SWT is the Most Merciful.

19

Love Note # 19: Life is about Avoiding Sins

Dear Priceless Princess,

Every day of our lives, we have to face many challenges whether it is a small problem or maybe a big dilemma. All these challenges are in a form to test one's patience and faith. Naturally, in our life, we are always guided by the do's and don'ts for us to be able to distinguish between right and wrong. Similarly, to live as a Muslim, we are always being tested by *Allah* SWT to see whether we abide by His rules or not.

The *do's* are the pillars of Faith and Islam and other good deeds we are encouraged to do, or must do such as eating and drinking lawful food.

Allah SWT said: "So eat of the lawful food and good food which *Allah* SWT has provided for you, and thank the bounty of your Lord if it is Him you serve." *Surah An-Nahl*, Verse 114.

And He also said: "He has forbidden for you only carrion and blood and swine flesh and that which has been sanctified in the name of any other than *Allah* SWT; but he who is driven to it, neither craving nor transgressing, then *Allah* SWT is Forgiving, Merciful." *Surah An-Nahl*, Verse 115.

There are also many things that we must avoid so that we do not gain sins. In Islam, there are seven major sins that a person must never commit, as explained by the Prophet Muhammad SAW.

In the name of *Allah* SWT, Most Gracious, Most Merciful.

Narrated by Abu-Huraira (may *Allah* SWT be pleased with him); 'The Prophet SAW said: "Avoid the seven great destructive sins."

The people enquired; 'O *Allah* SWT's Messenger! What are they?'

The Prophet *SAW*, said:

1. To join others in worship along with *Allah SWT*.
2. To practise sorcery.
3. To kill the life that *Allah SWT* has forbidden except for a just cause (according to Islamic law)
4. To eat up usury.
5. To eat up the orphan's wealth.
6. To show one's back to the enemy and fleeing from the battlefield at the time of fighting,
7. To accuse the chaste women, who never even thinks of anything touching their chastity and are good believers." *Hadith – Bukhari.*

These seven sins are grave indeed and must be avoided to gain *Allah SWT*'s pleasure.

20

Love Note # 20: Life is about Cleanliness

Dear Priceless Princess,

Life as a Muslim involves cleanliness in everything we do. It is an important part of a Muslim's daily practice and is compulsory to take care of, especially before performing a prayer or reading the Qur'aan. As a Muslim, you should:

- Make sure you are clean.
- Your clothes are clean from dirt.
- Your house is clean.
- Your school/office is clean.
- Your neighbourhood is clean.

We must practise cleanliness at all times, whether we are at home or outside. Of course we cannot always be clean during activities at work or home when times are busy, that would be unrealistic. However we should strive to acheive the best we can when it comes to cleanliness.

Without cleanliness, our prayers will not be counted. Our Prophet Muhammad *SAW* strongly encouraged us to be clean, therefore we follow his teachings.

21

Love Note # 21: Life is about Choosing Good Friends

Dear Priceless Princess,

The Prophet Muhammad *SAW* said that:

- Being friends with a good person is like being close to a perfume seller. If we were not sprayed with the pleasantly smelling perfume, we can still smell the pleasant aroma.
- Being friends with a bad person is like being near a goldsmith. If we were not sprayed with the flames from the fire, we will still inhale the smoke and stench.
- A person's behaviour depends on his/her friends' religion.

Be careful about whom you befriend! Friends also determine our success in this world. It's okay to choose friends carefully, as they will be the ones who guide us to the right or wrong paths. Having a wide circle of friends will allow you to learn much more about other faiths and cultures, it is important to always explain to friends how being a Muslim has its own way of life. One which can be shared and celebrated amongst all.

22

Love Note # 22: Life is about Choosing a Good Job

Dear Priceless Princess,

In Islam, it is essential for us to choose the right job so that we work for the right reasons and gain advantages from it. There is a certain guideline in choosing a job. Below is a quick list of things which are forbidden, *Haram*.

Examples:

- Do not get involved in a job that is associated with gambling.
- Do not get a job that is associated with liquor, whether it is the manufacturing of alcohol, distributing or selling a product that contains liquor.
- Do not get involved in any job that is associated with profit making that involves interest.
- Do not get involved in any job that is associated with stealing.
- Do not get involved in any job that is associated with adultery.

There are many great professions and jobs that we can choose from that can be productive for the wider society we live in and give us a source of *halal* means of making a living.

23

Love Note # 23:

Life is about Reciting Prayer

Dear Priceless Princess,

At any time, for whatever reason you want, recite a prayer to *Allah* SWT. As *Allah* SWT said: "And your Lord has said: Pray to Me and I will hear your prayer. Those who despise My service, they will enter hell, disgraced." *Surah Al-Mu'min*, Verse 60.

And our Prophet Muhammad SAW said:

- "Prayer is a weapon for a Muslim."
- "Prayer is the gist of worship to *Allah* SWT." *Bukhari and Muslim.*

Here are some useful prayers to know. Recite this to establish your worship to *Allah* SWT. "My Lord! Make me establish proper worship, and some of my posterity (also); our Lord! and accept my prayer." *Surah Ibrahim*, Verse 40.

Recite this to establish your forgiveness from *Allah* SWT. "On no soul doth Allah place a burden greater than it can bear. It gets every good that it earns and it suffers every ill that it earns. (Pray): "Our Lord! condemn us not if we forget or fall into error; our Lord! Lay not on us a burden like that which Thou didst lay on those before us; Our Lord! lay not on us a burden greater than we have strength to bear. Blot out our sins and grant us forgiveness. Have mercy on us. Thou art our Protector; help us against those who stand against faith." *Surah Al-Baqarah*, Verse 286.

Recite prayer for your parents."Our Lord! Forgive me and my parents and believers on the day when the account is cast." *Surah Ibrahim*, Verse 41.

Never forget to recite your prayers night and day. Truly, *Allah* SWT loves those who ask a favour from him and surely He will grant your wishes. A prayer can be recited in any language you like, because *Allah* SWT knows and hears all your prayers, regardless of language. He is the All-Knowing!

24

Love Note # 24:

Life is about Reciting the Qur'aan

Dear Priceless Princess,

Reciting the Qur'aan brings many advantages to all Muslims. By reading the Qur'aan, one can gain inner peace and open their hearts to good knowledge.

Because *Allah* SWT said: "Establish worship at the going down of the sun until the dark of night. And the recital of Qur'aan at dawn. The recital of Qur'aan at dawn is ever witnessed." *Surah Bani Israil*, Verse 78.

25

Love Note # 25: Last But Not Least

Dear Priceless Princess,

To me, you are my priceless TREASURE.

Wherever you go, whatever you do, I'm always thinking of you. I hope that you will always remember everything in this book and pass the knowledge to your children, your grandchildren and so on. I am always praying for your happiness in both this world and in the Hereafter.

Insha-*Allah* SWT.

Love,
Mom

About the Author

Tell us a little bit about yourself.
For twenty years, I have had an ambition to become a writer. It had always been my goal throughout the years and, despite English being my second language, I never gave up. My main focus is on providing Islamic material which parents, educators and children can relate to, without feeling overwhelmed.

What inspired you to write *A Priceless Princess?*
All parents worry about the challenges their daughters and sons will face. Being Muslim brings its own set of unique hurdles to address also. This idea originally led to writing little notes for my children, reminding them to always be faithful to their religion. Those notes are what inspired me to write this book. The book contains many short verses from the Qu'raan. They can be discussion points for the child and parent. This then shifts the focus from a child simply being told they cannot do something to trying to understand together with the parent the overall message of a Muslim's way of life.

What main message do you wish to give to readers when they read this book?
The main message from this book is to show them a new way of thinking and teach them the very basics of Islam. This book will hopefully serve as a short guide.

How will parents find this book useful when reading to children?
Parents are able to deliver the message of Islam in a form of language that is easy and understandable for young teens. This book will make it easier for them to distinguish between right and wrong and have a visualization on how to strategize our short life in this world.

When choosing themes to work on, how do you develop your ideas when writing?
Most of my ideas come from inspiration from my children in everyday life. I also developed them after reciting the Qur'aan.

What are you reading right now?
Getting Away with It, by Julie Cohen.

What was your favourite book as a child?
I have always been a fan of Enid Blyton when I was younger. I've enjoyed reading every one of her books so it's hard to pick a favourite!

If you could be any character in a book, who would you choose?
Tracy Beaker from *The Story of Tracy Beaker* written by Jacqueline Wilson because she is witty and fearless!

What other subjects would you like to write about?
I would like to specialize in the subject that relates the Qur'aan with the twenty-first century.

Do you have a favourite illustrator?
Nick Sharratt and Jeff Kinney.

When you are not writing how do you spend your time?
I'm busy juggling between teaching, researching and parenting.

What advice would you give to aspiring writers?
Have dreams! You'll discover that Allah is listening to each of your dreams and will grant your wishes if you work hard for it. Also, write whatever is on your mind and be inspired by everyday life.

What type of subjects would you like to see in today's Islamic literature market?
Any stories or Islamic materials that looks contemporary inside and outside. A book which is capable of capturing our children's young hearts in this new era in a way that is easy to deliver.